REPORT

OF THE

PROCEEDINGS OF A MEETING

HELD AT CONCERT HALL,

PHILADELPHIA,

On Tuesday Evening, November 3, 1863,

TO TAKE INTO CONSIDERATION THE CONDITION

OF THE

FREED PEOPLE OF THE SOUTH.

PHILADELPHIA:
MERRIHEW & THOMPSON, PRINTERS,
No. 243 Arch Street.
1863.

REPORT.

On motion of Stephen Colwell, Esq., President of the "Pennsylvania Freedmen's Relief Association," the Right Rev. Bishop Potter was called to the Chair, and Mr. J. Miller McKim and Mr. Ellis Yarnall were appointed Secretaries.

At the request of the Chairman, the Proceedings were opened by prayer, by the Rev. Dr. Spear.

Bishop Potter then said:

Ladies and Gentlemen:

I need not state the object for which we are assembled. Some eighteen months since the first public meeting was held in this city to consider the necessities of those people of African descent who, on the coast of South Carolina, had been separated from their masters and from their accustomed employments and support, by the fortunes of war. That meeting was followed by systematic arrangements, and by generous contributions for their physical wants and their moral and religious training.

Since then this class of persons has greatly multiplied. Along our whole Southern coast, from Fortress Monroe to St. Augustine, at the mouth and on both banks of the Mississippi, on the Tennessee and Cumberland and over immense tracts of country, they have been liberated and thrown, without guide or friend, upon the world. Under circumstances most demoralizing and, in many respects, most discouraging, this long suffering race have been on their trial; their temper, their capacity, their virtue,—all have been subjected to the severest strain. And who shall say that, considering their past disabilities and their sore temptations, they have not borne the trial nobly? Who shall say that they will not work, save when under the driver's lash? or that they are insensible to kindness? or that they can attain to no forecast and frugality in their affairs? or that they are slaves of vindictiveness? or that they are insensible to the value of rational freedom? In the camp and the battlefield they are fast vindicating their capacity for discipline, their unflinching courage, and their enthusiastic attachment to their whole country and to liberty. Honor, then, to the gracious Providence which has so wondrously opened to these people the path not only to nominal freedom but to real manhood. Honor to the readiness and the severe self-restraint and self control with which they have accepted the opportunity. Honor to the sympathy and generous kindness with which they have been relieved by many Christian hearts, and to the promptness with which cruel prejudice has, in numberless instances, given way before their advance to a higher life. And honor to you, my friends, that you do not shrink from the magnitude of their wants, but have come here prepared to consider and to help relieve them.

I hold in my hand a letter from a man whom to know is to love and whom we all honor and admire—Admiral Dupont. For many months he was in intimate relations, at Port Royal and elsewhere, with these people and with those who went to their relief. Let me read his testimony:

NEAR WILMINGTON, DELAWARE
29th OCT. 1863.

RT. REV. AND DEAR SIR:

I have your favor of this morning in reference to the operations of the Relief Committee raised in your neighborhood to help the blacks about Port Royal and the adjacent coasts.

It gives me pleasure to state that the relief sent to that region by humane and philanthropic individuals, through the Freedmen's Society and its committees, so far as it came under my observation, (and I had some opportunity of forming an opinion,) was judiciously applied and relieved most worthy objects from extreme want and destitution.

Supplies in food and raiment were followed by instruction in social organization, improvement in personal habits, in moral and religious teaching and the establishment of schools.

The conduct of the blacks as a whole was excellent. They appeared to appreciate all that was doing for them, and, with their first necessities relieved, I consider them quite capable of self support. They are not without industry; the spirit of freedom is very strong in them, the love of locality nearly as great, and they are extremely alive to the ties of relationship; they are, moreover, emotional and open to religious impressions, and very free from feelings of vindictiveness in reference to their past servitude.

I received yesterday a letter from a gentleman in Beaufort, S. C., who has been earnestly engaged in promoting the spiritual and physical welfare of this race; he tells me, "The people are improving; the crops are coming on well. If the tax commissioners get the lands into market in season, most of them will be bought by the Freedmen."

Believe me Rt. Rev. and dear Sir,

With the highest respect,

Your friend and humble servant,

S. T. DuPont.

Rt. Rev. Alonzo Potter, &c. &c.
Philadelphia.

I will detain you no longer. The case is assuming an extent and grandeur which demand immediate and organized treatment. The suffering of women and children especially require instant succour. We are fortunate in having with us a gentleman (Rev. Mr. Fiske) who has passed a long time in ministering to these people near Memphis, Tenn., and who will present you with the results of his experience.

The Chairman then introduced the Rev. A. S. Fiske, Chaplain of the Fourth Minnesota Regiment, who, for the last ten months, has been in charge of the "Contraband Camp" at Memphis, Tenn., and who now visits the North at the suggestion of Major-General Grant, and by order of the Superintendent in Chief of Contrabands in the Southwest, to make known the condition of the freed people of that region. Mr. Fiske spoke substantially as follows:

Having alluded to the patriotism and liberality of our people, explained his own position and the authority by which he was sent North upon his present mission, the duty enjoined upon him was to make known, as widely as possible, the necessities of the freedmen of the Southwest.

The care of these people was ours inevitably, from the moment we accepted the sword as the defenders of the Constitution. Prejudice and hate might repel for a time loyal men, with a mighty motive in their loyalty, from our lines. Or pride might reject aid from a despised race, though familiar with the field of conflict, and reared in the climate to which our sons and brothers too succumbed. But when the conflict grew hot and heavy, and the sacrifice was slain upon every household altar, common sense was soon to assume the sway. Before we accepted them, they were, as servants, bearing the army's burdens. and doing much of its work, as guides leading our scouts and reconnoissances, as spies bringing otherwise impossible information to our Generals, and gathering into camps all along our lines. In the course of Divine Providence, the care was on us, and could not be turned off, save by turning these people at wholesale, by starvation and nakedness, into graves.

Three-fourths of all the people who are now a burden upon the country would have been so under any conceivable war policy. They are the infirm and helpless, the women and children, abandoned upon plantations which had been stripped of everything that could sustain life. The effect of the Proclamation has been to induce many able-bodied men to effect their escape to our lines, who else would have been taken to the interior by their masters. It has not much increased our burdens, while it has vastly swelled the numbers of those who will do good service in arms.

There will be fifty thousand black soldiers in the field during the present winter, and at least as many more employed in the various fatigue duties of the service.

But there is another army equal to that in the Southwest, greater far than that, including the whole country, which we are to consider to-night. There rest this night in crowded camps from Helena to Natchez, on the Mississippi, not less than thirty-five thousand blacks, from whom all the able-bodied men have been assorted. Their shelter is old tents. A cheap ration is furnished by the government, which also turns over unserviceable military clothing for the infirm men. Officers—till recently chaplains—are detailed from the army to take charge of them, and to organize them for labor, when it can be found for them.

The speaker said: "I shall have some hard things to say of some of our officers and army, but in the midst of them all, let him, the modest, unpretending hero of Vicksburg, stand spotless. Overcoming early all prejudices of education and political training, he has stood the black man's friend. All that he could do he has done liberally, nobly. By his authority every measure for their care, protection and supply has been taken. The honor of his action in these affairs shall brighten forever the lustre of his enviable fame. This patriot hero shall be greeted as he lives on through the ages of the world's history as not only great but good."

He described the shameful abandonment of black men—too sick to move—in deserted camps, by our army, to perish alone in storm and mid-winter, stating that in one of its marches it left behind as many as forty of them to perish hopelessly. He described their suffering in a heavy snowstorm last winter, which resulted in the miserable deaths of many.

The key to all their dreadful destitution would be found in the manner of their coming in. They were abandoned by their masters on the approach of the Union army, refusing to follow them to the interior. The army living upon the country stripped their plantations of all eatable things, and left them no alternative but to go with the army or starve. There was nothing to be done but the able-bodied men must carry soldiers' loads; the women must gather up their children; the old men and women gather a little of their poor "dunnage," as they call it, and tramp on with the moving army. There is no help. Life thus—starvation else. Or, finding that the master proposes to take to the interior his able-bodied hands, leaving behind the women, who are for the present worthless, the able-bodied anticipate him, and gather the whole kindred, and try flight to the Union lines, pursued often by men and dogs. Happy if they can come in with their heart treasures safe, though destitute of winter supplies. Often, alas! the father comes alone, with the cry of wife and children ringing in his ears as they were taken back to bonds. What of them? God knows! By and by, he—this thing, wonderfully imitative, but no man—will go back to try again with and for them that fearful flight—this thing, that is no man, and has no heart, but is fit only to be owned and bought and sold and damned to his master's greed or lust!

The blacks of Jeff. and Joe Davis came in near Vicksburg in June last, and were supplied in their destitution with comfortables and the like, procured by the speaker from the agent of the Sanitary Commission. In this case they left their plantations with teams and plenty, but were stripped of all at the outposts of our army, and sent on to their camp as destitute as if they had started with nothing.

At Memphis alone, during the months of February, March and April, not less than twelve hundred colored people were buried in great pits, ten to twenty together, without coffin or shroud, and with scarcely clothing enough for decency. During this time there were in the vicinity about an average of four thousand of these people. They were in extreme destitution, many of them having but a single garment between them and nakedness. Few of them had bedding; they were sheltered in leaky tents, had no floors, and were but poorly supplied with cooking utensils, and had no arrangements for fires except outside their tents. The mortality among them was mainly the result of exposure in insufficient clothing.

The speaker dwelt at some length upon the prejudice existing against this people among Northern men, as illustrated in the conduct of our army toward them, giving many instances of extreme cruelty on the part of both officers and men. This spirit is, however, much changed, during the last six months, for the better, mainly through the arming of the blacks, and their great usefulness, beside, in fatigue duty.

Will these people work? Let facts reply. The Memphis camps have averaged about twenty-two hundred people. For the past five months the able-bodied men have been mainly on guard duty, maintaining themselves by wood-cutting the days they are off duty. Yet about four hundred comfortable log cabins have been built by them. Many thousand days' work for the government has been performed; two hundred and fifty acres of land cultivated, and three thousand cords of wood cut, and that for the most part with neither wages paid or promised.

They are cheerful, contented, industrious, and less improvident than could be expected.

But these abandoned people are unable to support themselves by regular cultivation of the soil. The wide belt of territory, lately devastated by the war, is still constantly overrun by guerrilla bands, who drive off or kill every negro who attempts to work upon it. Not a week passes but that parties of these maurauders sweep in within three miles of Memphis.

An interesting account was given of the grand marriage of the people, on the day of Thanksgiving for the victories of the summer. One hundred and fifteen couples were lawfully married that day in the camps, some of whom had lived together forty years, and had sons married, besides, the same day.

Their religion is rather one of feeling and passion, of extacies and visions than of holy living, as might be expected when it was taught them by those who could not apply it against any one of the practical vices of slavery. They learn eagerly and easily.

What is to be done with them? The speaker declared that they could not be sent north. They wouldn't concur. They would not leave the country. They could not be remanded to their masters. The work to be done is in the South. They are accustomed and willing to do it. Only let the government protect them as free men—give them the right to sell their labor in the best market—the right to learn; the right to own and inherit; the right to wife and children. and to do what they are able to do, and you need not trouble statesmen or politicians about their future. Reports of their sufferings have gone back through the confederacy and prevent them from coming in as they did six months ago. If it prove by and by that the rebels are able to arm the blacks against us, these reports alone will enable them to do it.

The speaker closed with an earnest appeal for a great national movement for the relief of the freed women and children in all departments.

Mr. Fiske was followed by Mr. J. Miller McKim, who said:

Mr. Chairman, I hold in my hands some resolutions, which, on behalf of the parties who have convoked this meeting, I desire to offer. Before reading them, I beg leave to make a few remarks:

About eighteen months ago, as you have intimated, sir, a meeting was held in this city similar in character and purpose to this. It was called to meet a pressing necessity. Our victorious arms in South Carolina had given us our first instalment of freedom, in the way of liberated slaves. Ten thousand human chattels, deserted by there fugacious masters, were thrown upon the country for maintenance and protection. They were in a most destitute condition, perishing for want of food and lack of needful clothing. An appeal in their behalf was made to Northern philanthropy by officers in command of the army and navy of the Southern Department. That appeal was responded to with promptness and liberality; and nowhere, I am proud to say, with more promptness and liberality than here in Philadelphia. The meeting referred to was called to consider the subject. You will well remember the occasion sir, for it was our good fortune then, as it is now, to have you for our presiding officer. Earnest addresses were delivered by speakers who set forth fully the whole subject. The people were moved. They adopted a resolution that these suffering blacks of the sea islands should have the relief—physical, mental and moral—which their necessities called for, and appointed a Committee to reduce this resolution to practice. That Committee—known afterwards as the "Port Royal Relief Committee," now styled, from its enlarged sphere, the "Pennsylvania Freedmen's Relief Association"—cheerfully undertook the task assigned it. How that task was executed, it is not for one speaking on its behalf to say. Its reports are before the public. They have been circulated extensively in this country, and republished abroad.

It is due, however, to the people of Philadelphia,—to those who gave character and shape to the meeting,—to say that the resolution adopted was no mere idle flourish. It was the expression of a fixed purpose; a purpose that was to be followed by corresponding action. At once contributions began to flow into the treasury of the Committee. With these, food and raiment were purchased and forwarded to the objects to be relieved. These again were followed by teachers and superintendents,—high-toned and devoted men and women,—whose labors from that time to this have been the admiration of the country,—have elicited grateful acknowledgments from the heads of the Government, and have reflected honor upon our national character among the people of foreign lands.

For, Mr. Chairman, this Port Royal business, though in itself considered a mere incident in the progress of the war—a mere episode in the history of our national struggle, is, nevertheless, in its bearings and relations, a matter of the very greatest moral and political significance. The Port Royal Experiment, as it has been called, has been a beacon light on the dark coast of our tempest-tossed political sea. It has revealed the only safe channel through which our imperilled ship of State could make its destined port. It has been one of the most beautiful of all that series of beautiful providences, by which the Good God has been leading us along,—saving us, as a nation, in spite of ourselves, from the rocks and reefs on which our sin-begotten prejudices against a race, and an insane and sorcerous attachment to slavery, were continually threatening to wreck us.

Port Royal, sir, has been to this country, and not to this country alone, a great and beneficent revelator. It has disclosed a wealth of virtue on the part of the people,—a latent mine of benevolence and love of impartial justice—previously unknown, and by many not even suspected. When, Mr. Chairman, at that meeting eighteen months ago, you, as its organ said, "the blacks of the sea-islands are perishing, and need immediate relief," the instant and emphatic reply was, "*they shall have it.*" The next day, in the Corn Exchange, gentlemen raised, for this object, a thousand dollars. This was followed by other thousands from other sources. Men and women, more than could be employed, volunteered as teachers and helpers.

Here was a revelation. As, in the beginning of the war, strong men, by thousands and tens of thousands, volunteered to fight,—to do the work of destruction made necessary by the rebellion,—so now it was seen that a noble army of men and women, stood ready to volunteer to do the moral work—the work of construction made necessary by the *cause* of the rebellion.

Port Royal has also brought to light a great wealth of resource possessed by the country, in the character and capabilities of the black man. That the blacks will work, without the whip, quietly, industriously, and that for the merest modicum of wages, the most reluctant are now compelled to admit. That they will fight, with the same bravery and the same skill as white men, and that they may be relied upon as defenders of our common country in time of war, has been made equally patent. Gen. Hunter's black regiment of South Carolina, were the first to put this fact beyond a peradventure. That they are susceptible to educational influences, the Port Royal enterprize has also placed beyond the possibility of cavil. Read the published testimony of teachers who have gone out from this city. Read the letters of that most accomplished and devoted lady, Miss Laura Towne; or those of the equally accomplished and devoted Miss Charlotte Forten, granddaughter of the late James Forten, of this city; or those of the estimable Mrs. General Saxton, formerly Miss Matilda Thompson, who went to South Carolina under the auspices of our Philadelphia Relief Committee.

But I need not multiply illustrations of what has been developed by this great Port Royal movement. Suffice it to say, its history constitutes one of the most instructive chapters in the annals of our country. It is a chapter that has been read, studied and reproduced in England and France, and that with the greatest advantage to our national cause, and to the cause of popular liberty everywhere.

Now, Mr. Chairman, for the moral of these statements: What has been done at Port Royal, can be done at Memphis. What can be done for South Carolina, can be done for Tennessee; and what can be done for both these States, can and ought to be done for all the other States of the South similarly situated.

What if there be "35,000 freed people on the banks of the Mississippi" looking to us for aid? What if there, and elsewhere, this number be increased, as it soon necessarily will be, tenfold? The more of them the better. The sooner they are all free, the sooner will the war be over; the sooner will the rebellion be suppressed, permanent peace restored, and the work of our national regeneration complete.

The resolutions I proposed to offer are as follows:

Whereas, We have heard with deep and painful interest the recitals which have been made to us of the condition of the freed blacks in

Tennessee, on the banks of the Mississippi, and elsewhere; and whereas, the destitution thus disclosed is of the most pressing exigency, making appeals which admit of no postponement; and whereas, it would be plainly unreasonable to demand of the Government—with a colossal war on its hands, and difficulties to contend with of unprecedented magnitude—that it should assume the entire burden of the support and management of this hapless people: therefore,

Resolved, That all citizens of the United States, and especially the loyal and humane of the North, owe a duty to the freed blacks of the South in their present distress, which demands immediate practical acknowledgement.

Resolved, That the necessities of these people, being inevitably incident to their transition from slavery to freedom, and the result of circumstances for which they are in nowise responsible, ought to be, and must be, provided for by those on whom, by their own assumption, this responsibility rests.

Resolved, That the extent and probable duration of the state of things which now makes its appeal to us, forbid the idea of meeting it by any mere local, extemporaneous, or impulsive effort; but that, on the contrary, they demand that it should be provided for by a well digested and carefully organized system of general operations; and that we recommend that immediate steps be taken by parties interested in the subject in this city, to put on foot a plan of concerted action, the scope of which shall be coextensive with the country; and the results, a proper provision for the necessities, mental, moral, and physical, of all who may justly claim its benefits.

Resolved, That in the meantime the people of Philadelphia and of the State of Pennsylvania should come forward with their accustomed liberality to meet the present exigency, and that, besides contributions in clothing to supply the demand now made upon them, a sum not less than $50,000 should be raised for the purpose of carrying out the object of this meeting.

I am reluctant to trench upon the time of the speaker who is to follow me, whom I am sure you are impatient to hear, but I beg the privilege of a few additional words, suggested by these resolutions.

It is asserted that it would be unreasonable to demand that the government, burdened as it is, should assume the entire *onus* of looking after the welfare of these people. Mr. Chairman, I am in favor of holding our public servants to a strict account; but there is such a thing as exacting too much. It would not be possible for any government to pass safely through the difficulties which environ ours, without the largest amount of outside popular assistance. I doubt, sir, if there be another government now on the face of the earth, that could bear up under the burdens which now press upon the broad shoulders of this. Our integrity as a nation at this moment, maintained in spite of the prophecies of Europe's wisest men, is due to the elastic nature of our institutions; to the democratic form, under which power, in this country, is administered.

It is our duty, sir—the duty of every loyal citizen—to come up to the help of the government in this great crisis, and I rejoice to know that the people recognize the duty. Look at the Sanitary Commission, with its hundreds of faithful workers and its $7,000,000 disbursed for the benefit of the suffering and wounded! Look at the Christian Commission, with similar instrumentalities, spending money like water for the same purposes! Look at the numerous other voluntary, outside associations got up to support the government in its hour of trial!

Now, Mr. Chairman, the greatest want of all, at the present moment, is—as these resolutions point out—a well organized and widely extended system of operations for the benefit of the freed men. It is recommended here, that steps toward such an organization be immediately taken. Shall it be done? If so, by whom? Shall we wait, as has been our bad habit in times past, for New York or Boston to take the initiative? Why should Philadelphia wait for the lead of either of these cities? Let us be true to our traditions. This city has always been distinguished, and justly, for its broad charities; its wide-reaching humanity. Look at our numerous well endowed hospitals, of every variety and for every class. Look at our Volunteer Refreshment Saloons, feeding, without money and without price, hundreds of thousands of our country's brave defenders. Look at the Union League giving $300,000 to support and defend the government. Look at our Volunteer Enlistment Committees, one of them disbursing a bounty fund of $500,000, all contributed voluntarily by citizens of Philadelphia; another, in the teeth of prejudice, assuming the responsibility and expense of putting into the field, three regiments of black U. S. troops; and, having nearly completed this task, now holding itself ready to do three times as much more in the same direction.

Mr. Chairman, I say not these things to flatter, I say them as a basis of an argument. Let us be true to our traditions. Let Philadelphia be true to her historic character. She is rich; the State is prosperous; the whole North is plethoric with abundance; out of this abundance let us give.

Sir, I think the sum fixed in the resolutions too small. Fifty thousand dollars is not enough for so great a city, in so great a cause. I will take the liberty, therefore, of suggesting that the resolutions should read "not less than one hundred thousand dollars."

The chairman introduced to the audience the Rev. Phillips Brooks, who spoke in effect as follows:

We are not dealing to-night with an entirely new subject. One of the most remarkable things about our time is the way in which experience is matured now in periods that we used to think wholly inadequate. We used to need years to learn lessons that months can teach us now. And so, although this work of the Freedmen's relief is only two years old, we have certain clear ideas about the way it ought to be conducted, and the method of its success. The change of name of this Committee is significant Starting as the "Port Royal Relief Committee," it widens its view now, and becomes the "Freedmen's Relief Association." Called to enter on a wider sphere of action, it carries with it the history of that Port Royal enterprise for a continual incitement and direction. That enterprise, growing out of the capture of Hilton Head by Com. Dupont, just two years ago this week, presents us certain well-ascertained results, which we set down as facts. It has proved that the freed black man is capable of a will to work, a desire to learn, an appreciation of liberty, a healthy social ambition, and a very practical and effective religion. It has proved, moreover, that he is capable of, and may be made to manifest all these, not in a small, but in a very large degree; that when you eliminate the necessary conditions which he lacks, and make account of the disadvantages under which he labors, his progress has been very remarkable indeed. For you have to eliminate those things which help the free worker at the North, but are wanting to the freed worker at the South. First, a traditionary habit of labor; second, an inciting public opinion; third, hereditary dispositions and ambitions; and you have to add these things which hinder the laborer at Port Royal, but not the laborer in Pennsylvania; 1st, an undefined social condition; 2d, an insecure hold on the results of labor; 3d, the contempt and discouragement of many who ought to help him; 4th, a bad climate; 5th, a bad training and a blood only one or two generations removed from savage life. Keep these things in mind, and then read the reports of this Port Royal work and weigh its results, and you will grant that it has proved the true *method* of this problem of the Freedman's destiny.

The true *method* has been proved but nothing more. To make that *method* effective is the immense work that is opening before us now. The people have led the Government in the good work of Emancipation; now it does not become them to leave that government unsustained in the inevitable consequences of that work for which we thank God.

We call on the people to accept the immense fact of these thousands of helpless black people, and without being deterred by the old prejudice of race, or the endlessness of the toil, to come forward and assume it as one of the burdens of this generation.

We call on you on broader grounds—not as anti-slavery men, not even as Americans, but just as men whose brethren are sick, and naked, and hungry, and cold, and ignorant; we appeal for food, and clothes, and teachers, to send them, in the name of their share in the humanity of Him who said—"Whatsoever ye would that men should do to you, do you even so to them."

At the conclusion of Mr. Brooks' speech, Mr. McKim, as one of the Secretaries, announced that the names of five gentlemen had just been handed up as contributors; four of them subscribing a thousand dollars each, and the fifth, five hundred. "A good beginning," the speaker remarked, "toward the $100,000 recommended." The announcement was received with applause. It was further announced that Mr. Edward Clark, 35 S. Third Street, was Treasurer of the Freedmen's Association, and that all contributions in money should be sent to him; while donations in clothing, should be sent to the Counting-house of Mr. James A. Wright, an active member of the Association, No. 115 Walnut Street.

Before taking the question on the *Resolutions*, Bishop Potter remarked that they presented two distinct and important subjects. 1st. The necessity of a national and efficient organization to meet the emergency created in respect to these people by the advance of our armies; and 2d, the raising at once in this city of $50,000 or $100,000 to supply the present necessities of the women and children. He hoped that Philadelphia would not forget what she owed, not only to the subject, but to her own past. It should be held in lively remembrance that in this city the doctrine of what we owed to the black man was for the first time distinctly and perseveringly proclaimed. More than an hundred and twelve years ago, a humble school master of Philadelphia, but one of the best and wisest of men,—Anthony Benezet—uttered the voice of true humanity and of Christian duty on this subject. It was at his feet that many years afterwards Thomas Clarkson learned the alphabet of his far-famed philanthropy. The place which contains the ashes of such an Apostle of charity should be forward in the good work, that is proposed this evening.

The meeting then adjourned.

ADDENDUM.

The object of the meeting, the proceedings of which are here reported, is not a partial one. This will have been perceived by the careful reader; but it is best, perhaps, that it should be distinctly stated.

The Pennsylvania Freedmen's Relief Association, who originated the meeting, contemplate the benefit, without preference, of all who may justly claim their offices. They have before them appeals from almost every Southern State. From Port Royal there still comes a demand for teachers and books. The more the blacks there learn, the more they want to learn. From the contraband camps at Washington and on Arlington Heights they have appeals for clothes and bedding as a protection against the approaching winter. From Fortress Monroe, a letter has been received from Mr Wilder, superintendent of the freed blacks, who is carrying on an agricultural experiment near that station, an extract from which is as follows:

"Our plantation operations are doing wonders, and in another year, if we can get farming implements and seed enough, we expect to astonish the best friends of the negro with our success. * * * Were it not for the old, and young, and sick, and feeble, and new comers, all of whom *have nothing*, and *need all things*, we would not be beggars, but givers. Schools and meetings are well attended and do a world of good."

From Nashville, Major Stearns sends a letter, the import of which will be gathered from the following:

We find in this city between twelve and eighteen hundred children, of twelve years of age and under, who are mostly of mixed blood, speaking the English language, intelligent, apt to learn, entering a sphere of self-dependence untried by their class as yet, that are to be rescued from a prospective condition of degradation and demoralization, only by the efforts of the benevolent. We propose to give our attention to the female portion of these children first, and could we obtain Two Thousand Dollars, added to what means could be obtained in this locality, we could make a beginning in this noble work.

From North Carolina an appeal comes to the Freedmen's Association in this city, in form as follows:

OFFICE OF THE EDUCATIONAL COMMISSION,
BOSTON, Nov. 6th, 1863.

Dear Sir:—The enclosed paper, extracts from letters from Mrs. James, wife of the 'Superintendent of Blacks,' at Newbern, has been laid before the Committee on Teachers. In sending so many teachers to Port Royal, Newbern, Norfolk, Alexandria and Georgetown, we use so much of the money subscribed to the commission, that the supply of clothing we can send can never meet the demand. The Philadelphia Society has worked so wisely and successfully at Port Royal, in establishing, by its store there, trade with the freed people in the articles they need, that it is thought best to send this paper to you, in the hope that your society may establish the same beneficent arrangement with the Newbern people. They have money, but they cannot pay the exhorbitant prices of the sutlers. Would it be agreeable to you to lay this matter before your Association, and inform us whether they think fit to take action upon it?

Respectfully, &c.

The "paper," referred to, contained the following:

August 29th.—At Howell's camp, over 1400, mostly women and children. Only a few instances among all these people where the family has any one on whom to depend, or any one to earn anything. Very many aged women, decrepit and infirm; some such have the care of two or three, in one instance of five grand-children. One such person has been in the camp four months, and has had in all this time but a single garment of her own; when needful to wash it, some woman, more fortunate, would lend her a covering. No shoe or stocking, *nothing* but this coarse ragged garment, of material not unlike crash. She had the care of four little children, "motherless young-uns missus," and was assiduous and faithful to them as far as possible. I took out three barrels closely packed with clothing, and two ladies to aid in the distribution, and we each felt, when through, that we had not *begun* to supply the most pressing wants.

We are besieged at the office with applications to buy supplies, as all trade is in the hands of sutlers, &c., and not a yard of material is obtainable under 30 to 45 cts., at the very lowest.

September 2d.—I have issued sixteen barrels of clothing since my return, and am now all out of supplies. There is a great demand for boys' clothing—boys from 8 to 14 years, who are very desirous to attend the schools, now going on so well, and yet are not sufficiently covered to be willing to present themselves. Many of these boys come with money that they have earned, and want to buy clothes, but we cannot supply them, and to buy materials of the suttlers is simply impossible; so the poor fellows must wait.

As I write the yard is filled with blacks, who seem to think that by waiting until they see me they can get some calico, although the clerk has told them that it is all gone.

September 24th.—The yard of the office is thronged daily with blacks, of all conditions, asking for clothing. Some have money to pay; some have notes from the superintendent of the camp where they live, stating that they are poor and have no work to do to earn anything, while others in squalid features and rags, that leave half their persons exposed, tell their own tale of poverty and wretchedness. I repeat what I have before stated to you, that my greatest discouragement is lack of clothing for gratuitous distribution.

The soldiers under Gen. Wild, now before Charleston, in many cases left families, and their wives, many of them, have nothing to clothe their little ones with in this damp season now coming upon us. These *peculiarly* claim our care.

At present I have not a garment of any kind either for sale or gratuity.

October 12th.—I find that these people who attend schools are at once desirous of something *whole*, in place of the rags that scarcely cover their persons, and *children*, especially, want clothes. They quickly become ashamed to associate with "de ladies," when they "has noting better dan dis yere," and "no shiftier close."

We are in want of dresses for girls, who are almost women, and for women who are pupils. In issuing our supplies I give preference to pupils of the ladies, who are out here, as well as to the pupils of Mrs. Doolittle, after that to the soldiers families. Many women are waiting for a frock before they can enter a school. They come to me with their sad story, and say at the close, "de teacher says we's mus come all *clean*, an now missus I'se can't be clean wi noting but dis yere old rag." The proposition is self-evident, and when, as is often the case, the applicant has in her hand 50 or 75 cents, and perhaps more, it is sad to turn her empty away. The checks which you sent us are on the persons of those who attend school every day or evening. It is pleasant to recognize them.

October 8th. Miss Chase.—Can you furnish me with knitting yarn and kneedles? Every colored foot is bare, and every colored woman can knit. You cannot send me too much yarn, so I will expect a great deal. If you have shoes for us, they would be very acceptable. The bare knees of hard-working men, whom I hoped were clothed for the winter, are even now looking out upon the day, and women are wanting petticoats, and everybody is asking for blankets.

Similar appeals are coming all the time from various parts of the Southern States. To all of these it is the purpose of the Association to respond impartially; aiding those first who are most necessitous and providing for all with such liberality as their means may warrant.

The Port Royal enterprise, to which the people of Philadelphia have so liberally contributed, has been in every respect successful. The freed people there are now a happy, thrifty, self-supporting community. Several of them are, in a small way, landed proprietors and planters. Their children go to school, and have already made such progress that some of them in their turn are now performing the part of assistant teachers.

In illustration as well as proof of these statements, take the following extract of a letter lately received from Mr. Reuben Tomlinson, of this city, now General Superintendent, under Government, of the Island of St. Helena:

"There never was a time, when every thing connected with our enterprize here seemed to me more promising than now. So far as plantation labor is concerned, we are just in the midst of harvest, and all the crops are good. Indeed the cotton crop will be, I think, larger and better in all respects, than was anticipated by any of us a month ago. The 'crop' last year, *as such*, was so complete a failure, that we hardly dared to look forward to a much better one this year. I think we all felt that, owing to the people's dislike of 'Cotton,' and our ignorance of its proper culture, comparatively little could be done for some years. That we were mistaken in these prognostications, this year's harvest will prove. You will not understand from this, that I anticipate a yield equal to 'Secesh' times. Nothing of the sort. In the first place, there has not been more than half as much cotton planted, as was usual in the days of slavery. We have not laid ourselves out for the purpose of raising cotton, but to make the people self-supporting and independent. In this I have no doubt that we have succeeded; and we shall have raised enough cotton to pay all our expenses besides.

Hereafter, no person in this Department, excepting those that would be paupers under any circumstances, need draw a single 'ration' from Government. On this 'place' there is already double as much 'cotton' now picked, as was gathered during the whole season last year. And this I think is true of every other plantation. The cotton is also, in quality, very much superior to that of last year. * * *

In the Educational department the results are equally flattering. I do not get time to visit the schools as much as I would like to, but the observations that I have made lead me to but one conclusion, and that is that the progress made is truly marvellous.

The following letter, with some omissions to save space, is taken from the New York Tribune of the 9th of November:

From an Occasional Correspondent.

BEAUFORT, S. C., Nov. 4, 1863.

These Sea Islands have become a modern Goshen. The people, who long dwelt in darkness, now have "light in their dwellings," and "the cloud" resteth between them and their enemies.

The crops have been gathered, the laborer has been paid his hire, and yet the lash has not been used, nor the driver's horn been heard through all the season.

Statesmen, were they here, would find an answer to the question, so often asked, "What shall be done with the colored people?" Manufacturers, who have trembled lest their spindles should cease their music—merchants, who have stood aghast at the prospect of empty shelves—would dismiss their fears if they knew what is transpiring in these islands, the "Pahdees" may safely throw away the torch and the rope.

Now the call, the almost universal call, is for hands. The hard earnings and scanty savings of the season are to be invested in lands and a home. So intense has been the desire for land that nearly all have laid by something for a home.

The President, in his instructions to the Tax Commissioners, has provided that a certain proportion of the land shall be sold to none but freedmen, and in tracts not exceeding twenty acres, at $1 25 per acre. This provision is good, so far as it goes, but the real wants of the people require more.

That the people can support themselves all here admit. But can they govern themselves? is a question not yet solved satisfactorily to all. Well, we are to see. A little Republic has been formed in our great Republic. It is like the "wheel in a wheel" in Ezekiel's vision. "Squatter sovereignty" is the corner-stone. Like the pioneers of the prairies, anticipating the slow movements of the Government, and having confidence in each other, they have resolved to lay, each man, "his claim" to twenty acres, build him his house and enjoy life. When this matter was first named, some friends doubted the feasibility of it, but at a meeting recently held, where were gathered men and women who stood and sat in ranks of hundreds beneath the shadows of the beautiful pines, the fearful were made confident, and believers were confirmed. The day was the holy Sabbath; the place just outside a church, near the centre of Port Royal Island. There were present the Military Governor, Gen. Saxton and lady, Col. Van Wyck, 56th New York, and late M. C., and officers of various grades in the army and navy, Treasury and Plantation Agents, missionaries, and a large number of intelligent lady teachers and friends. Among the freedmen were scores upon scores of "field women," tidily clad, their smiling faces indicating that they had entered a new life. Hundreds of manly forms of fathers, husbands, brothers, who had once borne the crushing weight of Slavery, were there. The 1st South Carolina, Col. Higginson, had sent a delegation of noble men to claim the soldiers' right to a piece of land—a claim granted by Congress, and confirmed by their noble, heroic deeds as soldiers. The services opened by singing

"Children of a Heavenly King,
As we journey let us sing," &c.

Prayer was then offered by the Rev. Mr. Hall, (colored), from New York, after which the Rev. Mr. French addressed the people from these words: "Behold the Lord thy God hath set the land before thee; go up and possess it, as the Lord God of thy fathers hath said unto thee; fear not, neither be discouraged," Deut. i. 21.

General Saxton, large hearted and courageous in all that appertains to the good of his people, explained clearly to them the importance of their owning permanent homes. They were on trial now before themselves and the nation. He had full faith that they would succeed.

Rules for governing the people in settling upon and finally securing a title to the lands were then adopted.

These rules were preceded by the following declaration:

"We, the free colored people now residing in the Parish of St. Helena, in the State of South Carolina, pledging our lives and services, as far as we are capable, to the United States, and vowing loyalty to the same, and being desirous of vindicating our rights to freedom, and our claims to recognition as freemen, and of exhibiting to the world our capacity to maintain our position as such, and of evincing our gratitude to Almighty God, who has brought us out of the house of bondage, do hereby mutually covenant and agree with each other to observe, obey, adhere to and maintain the following rules and regulations."

Col. Van Wyck delivered a stirring address, and was followed by Serjeant Rivers, 1st South Carolina Volunteers, in a speech that made all hearts rejoice. He said:

"Gen. Hunter called him to be a soger. He was a recruiting officer. He started out Sabbath day, and got thirty-nine men befo' sundown. He was glad to be a soger, and he meant to knock at the door of the Union till he got his rights, or die knocking. He saw the womens all hold back der husbands, did n't want them to go sogering, 'cause they get killed. Women worse than the men, and some hide the men in the woods. Now you see, we gets our pay for going to the army. The Government lets we sogers have our land and pay one quarter down, and have three years to pay the rest. I feel 'shamed for our women. They ought to know the man's place is to take care of the women and children, else he be no man at all. If anybody hide, let the women hide, and the man stand out the door and see where the danger is. Now we sogers are men—men de first time in our lives, Now we can look our old masters in de face. They used to sell and whip us, and we did not dare say one word. Now we an't afraid, if they meet us, to run the bayonet through them. Now we help the

Government. The white soldiers used to say, the niggers fight! oh no, dem black niggers don't fight. Wont fight if they be sogers. Now they done cursing—they say, come on brother soldier, we will whip out the Rebels. My brethren, I don't intend to lay down my gun till the war is done, and our brethren all get their freedom—and then, if I be alive, I will come home and enjoy my family and my land. We mens, fifty of us in the 1st S. C., have got $1,000 for land, and I won't say how much more, but if any man bids against us, he will find we got another dollar more. So just let him remember that. And now, as you goes to pick your land, don't you men, who were afraid to go and fight, feel cowardly like the women; don't you go and pick all the best places. The old men, the weak ones, and the poor women must have the cleared land, and you take the woods. We fight the Rebels right up in Fort Wagner, where the bayonets were. Now you take the woods and work, and let the old ones, and the women, and the children, whose husbands and fathers are among the Rebels, have the good lands. For my part, I mean to stand by the agreement. Gen. Saxby our friend, and I mean to stand by him and work for the Lord."

Rarely was ever a speech made that did more honor to the speaker or afforded more pleasure to his audience. A model house was here exhibited, constructed of poles and without nails, such as Gen. Mitchell built for the people at Hilton Head before his death. Mr. Wilson is building these houses as rapidly as possible, with a large force of carpenters. They are 16 by 24, and cost about $25. The most of the people can build the houses for themselves. The people, in view of having homes of their own and home comforts, such as every heart yearns for, were carried away in transports of joy. In breaking up the meeting, the cordial greetings, the thanksgivings, the "Lord bless you, Massa," were like copious showers. The day was a jubilee.

The meeting adjourned, but not the action of the people. The islanders are like bees returning from a clover-blossomed field, laden with the rewards of diligent toil. From all quarters young men, middle-aged, and the old man, bending under the weight of fourscore years and ten, are coming into town with their money. None bring less than $25. Here comes from the ferry, twelve miles distant, an aged pilgrim, staff in hand, tidily clad, with a "twenty years younger, massa, since the meeting yesterday" on his lips, and lays down his wallet, saying, "please count dat, massa, dat for me and my old woman. We tankful to have home and freedom, if only one day, before we die."

Next comes a man saying "our people are thirty head; we be on the plantation; we get $500; we want all ole massa place. We work on it all our days. We support him, and well too; now we take care of ourselves. He welcome to raise de hominy, and have it all himself. We jist want to see how much cotton and corn we can raise."

The very latest intelligence that has been received from Port Royal is contained in the following extract from a letter of Mr. John Heacock, one of the Superintendents who went out under the direction of the Philadelphia Relief Committee:

WALKER'S PLANTATION,
Port Royal Island, Nov. 5, 1863.

The cotton crop is now nearly gathered; on this plantation there will be about 2,500 lbs. of ginned cotton. This will be about 100 lbs. to the acre, against 300–350 in secesh times. This falling off is to be attributed to the want of manure and the want of animals to do the necessary work. All last winter there was but one mule and a very poor cart upon this place. Then was the time to get the manure. We have now two mules and two carts. I hope next year to see double the crop. I think it can be done. The best acre so far has yielded 412 lbs., with enough probably remaining to make 500 lbs. It will be some time before northern people can make the crops that used to be made; there is so much to learn. I think the yield on this plantation is about an average.

☞ **What has been done at Port Royal, the Pennsylvania Freedmen's Relief Association purpose to do, to the extent of their means, in all the Southern States.**

www.ingramcontent.com/pod-product-compliance
Lightning Source LLC
LaVergne TN
LVHW011144110826
845150LV00008B/2508

* 9 7 8 1 4 1 8 1 9 2 0 0 6 *